AF539549

KAY RUSSELL ★ NANCY JONES

ILLUSTRATED BY BOB TAYLOR

EAKIN PRESS ★ BURNET, TEXAS

FIRST EDITION

Published in the United States of America
By Eakin Press, P.O. Drawer AG, Burnet, Texas 78611

ISBN 0-89015-314-0

Dedication

Phil Jones - Chris, Jane, and Tut

Russ Russell - Rusty and Mark

SPECIAL THANKS GO TO:

Johnnie Alambar
Betty Anderson
Billy Anderson
Susie August
Mary Lou Bobo
Monte Borders
Bob Brooks
Orval Browning
Frances Brougher
George Bumford
Jean Bumford
John C. Butler
Coit Carpenter
Donna Cox
Ronnie Crownover
Mary Jane Fields
Jack Glover
Mary Hager
Gary Hill
Bill Hudson
Frank Jones
Phil Jones
Larry Lilly
Bub Lofland
John Mazziotta
Tom Neely
Nub Neighbors
Harold Nelms
Donna New
Lucille Norwood
Howard Peterson
Virgil Pyles
Russ Russell
Cathy Schlegel
Tess Schlegel
Sallie Simpson
Andy Sisk
Bob Taylor
J.T. Tompkins
Andy Tuttle
Charlie Tuttle
Fred Tuttle
Clarence Vaughan
Darrah Mae Vaughan
Bill White
Ernestine White
Kemper Williams, Jr.

COWBOYS SAY IT BETTER ...

This book is written for the cowboy who has never seen a cow and the horseman who has never been on a horse. Cowboys are a vanishing breed, whose picturesque speech grew out of the solitary life on the vast, rough prairie. His language was a composite of the beauty, toughness and loneliness of the land around him. These mental and visual pictures were humorous, witty, and so descriptive. This is the language which eventually crept into every corner of Texas. Each region boasts of its own dialect, which has been passed from generation to generation.

As native Texans, we were raised on this "talkin'," and we felt a need to preserve at least a part of it. Our husbands, Russ and Phil, are masters of this speech in every sense and really were our inspiration in writing this book. We are indebted to them and to many relatives and friends who contributed to this endeavor.

Our interviews were a lot of fun and we met many Texas cowboys, young and old. We visited a domino parlor in a little Texas town, and a trading post in Sunset, Texas, run by a man who represents the last of a rare breed of cowboy. Jack Glover is a true character—author, sculptor, collector, and all around great guy. From the trading post we traveled to the busy streets of Dallas to interview Billy Fred, who in real life is Bill Hudson, president of the Valley View Bank. Billy Fred is a real Texas talkin' farmboy who writes a regular newsletter and is often heard on KVIL radio.

Another of our favorites was Tom Neely, resident cowboy and horse trainer at the Russell Ranch. When we asked him for some expressions, he'd reply, "I just can't think of any," but if we stood around for a few minutes he'd come through. His natural conversation is studded with real cowboy talk. Describing a bunch of horses might sound like, "that one's stacked like a brick outhouse," another one "treetop tall," and "he's longer than a well rope."

We know you will come up with some sayings of your own, and we hope you enjoy the book and are able to incorporate some of this talkin' into your everyday discussions. Our experiences convinced us that cowboys certainly do say it better—and you can, too!

The good Lord willin' and the creeks don't rise.

Longer than a well rope.

Scarce as hens' teeth.

Don't cut your foot. (Don't step in a cow patty).

Don't miss the water 'til the well runs dry.

You'd do to ride the river with.

My kind of cattle.

He's the first one you look for and the last one you'd want to meet.

Tall in the saddle.

Well done is better than well said.

Be on you like a duck on a June Bug.

He's like a duck—webfooted and doesn't give a damn.

She's always taken her ducks to a good market. (Refers to someone having good fortune in life.)

She dropped him like a bad habit.

I've been lookin' at the north end of a southbound mule all day. (Plowin')

Fiddlin' around.

You can't make a silk purse out of a sow's ear.

Sore hocked. (Foot or ankle trouble.)

Don't sweat the mule, just load the wagon.

He has more brass than an army mule.

He could tear up an anvil with a toothpick.

He couldn't hit a bull in the ass with a handful of gravel.

He couldn't hit a bull in the ass with a bass fiddle.

Kick up your heels.

His luck is runnin' kinda muddy.

He's one brick short of a load.

He's not pullin' a full train.

He's not playin' with a full deck.

He don't have both oars in the water.

He's cross threaded.

He's a little bit off plumb.

Look in her eyes and there's nobody home.

That's more than you can say grace over.

She's ridin' herd on a passel of young uns.

Like closing the barn door after the horse is out.

Sidewinder. (Rattlesnake)

Shoot the moon. (Bet it all)

Whistling like a lost freight.

Whistling like a ten penny nail.

The whole nine yards.

Drunk as a skunk.

Jake leg.

Drunk as a coot.

He drinks like he has a hollow leg.

Tight as a tick.

Tight as Dick's hatband.

Come hell or high water.

That's like trading the devil for the witch.

I've stacked my wood on worse.

Wake up if you want to make your dreams come true.

He made a bigger impression than a three-legged man at an ass kickin' contest.

He's in hog heaven.

Blacker than the inside of a cow.

She may be small, but she's wound tight.

He's as confused as a little boy who dropped his chewing gum in the chicken yard.

Spreadin' like a grass fire.

Grinnin' like a possum eatin' green persimmons.

Grinned like a jackass eatin' thistles.

Hell to pay.

All wool and a yard wide. (A fine person)

The mosquitoes are so big they use mousetraps to catch 'em.

Playin' possum.

That's like jumping from the skillet into the fire.

Hard as nails.

Sharp as a tack.

Racked my brain.

Chili is a bowl of fire, a bowl of red, or a bowl of green.

Don't give a flip or not worth a flip.

He would do to tie to.

Hell ain't half full.

You bet your boots.

Barkin' up the wrong tree.

Let's hightail it outa there.

Hamstrung. (At a disadvantage)

Sold his saddle. (Disgraced)

Hung up his saddle. (Died)

Buffaloed. (Bluffed)

Shake a rope at him. (Warn him)

Cow pasture pool.

That's like a pot callin' the kettle black.

The fat hits the fan. (Trouble)

I'd know your ashes in a whirlwind.

I'll spank you so hard you won't have anything but rags to shake.

No hill for a climber.

No hill for a stepper.

No step for a stepper.

He's catchin' em faster'n I can string 'em.

He's an accident lookin' for a place to happen.

What fur? Cat fur to make kitten britches. (None of your business)

Wings don't mean a chicken can fly.

Hide and watch.

Time flies when you're havin' fun.

You can't beat it with a stick.

I reckon.

Even a blind hog finds an acorn once in a while.

Mad as a puffed toad-frog.

Mad as a settin' hen.

She flew all over him like a banty hen.

I'm mad enough to eat burnt peanuts.

The shit hit the fan.

Mad enough to eat nails.

I'm so mad I could spit nails.

On the prod. (Mad, wanting to fight—refers to "cows on the prod")

Mad as a wet hen.

He threw a wall-eyed fit.

He got his dander up.

Don't that rile your innards!

Plumb riled.

He'd be mad if they hung him with a new rope.

Acts like he has a burr under his saddle.

Hotter'n a turpentine cat.

Lookin' for a dog to kick.

Anti-Godlin. (Old timers' description of going diagonally or in a round-about way.)

A little piece down the road or a fur piece down the road.

Whopper Jawed.

Catty Wampus. (Not in a straight line)

Just a stone's throw and a holler away.

Over "yonder."

Headin' home like a goose ridin' south on a cold norther.

Last time I saw him he was headin' south with a white rat in his mouth.

He's so ornery he'd push little ducks in the water.

Bad actor. (Mean cuss)

Cold blooded as a rattler with a chill.

He don't have no more conscience than a cow in a stampede.

He's a real scalawag. (Not worth much)

He's a lowdown sidewinder. (Snake)

Meaner'n a snake.

He ain't no account.

He's sorry enough to pour water on a poor widow woman's kindling.

I'll knock you clear into the middle of next week.

Lock horns.

Fought tooth and toe nail.

Cruisin' for a bruisin'.

Clean his plow. (Beat him up)

I'm gonna tan your hide.

Blow out his lamp. (Kill him)

Pistol whip. (Beat up)

I'm gonna get on your back so bad you're gonna have to burn up your best Sunday shirt to smoke yourself out from under me.

I'll kick your butt so high, you'll have to unbutton your pants to smile.

Lock, stock, and barrel.

Don't go off half-cocked.

A flash in the pan.

Fast on the trigger.

His gun has lots of notches.

Sure as shootin'.

Bite the bullet.

That's a square shootin' bunch of folks.

He's a real straight shooter.

He's not worth the powder it'd take to blow him to hell.

His Daddy was a pistol—he's a son of a gun.

Big fifty. (Buffalo Sharps gun)

He cut his teeth on a gun barrel.

Quick on the draw.

There's no use crying over spilt milk.

Cry in one hand and spit in the other and see which gets full first. (Stop crying)

I'm gonna get you a sugar titty.

Plumb tuckered out.

I feel like an empty shuck. (Tired)

Played out.

I feel like I've been chewed up and spit out.

I feel like I've been rode hard and put away wet.

Tougher'n a campfire steak.

He's so tough he uses prickly pear for a napkin.

Tough as a boot.

Tougher'n a burnt boot.

Too wild for the West and too fast for the movies.

He's so country his breath smells like cordwood.

As country as a dozen eggs.

As country as homemade soap.

Happy as a dead bird in the sunshine.

So thirsty I could spit cotton.

Bleedin' like a stuck pig.

Stingy brim (Small-brimmed hat)

He can run faster, jump higher, dive deeper, and come up drier than anyone else.

Cowboy cool. (Lukewarm)

His hair looked like it had been combed with a skillet.

He went out to get his mane roached. (Haircut)

Turkey trot.

I've known him since Heck was a pup.

Tough titty, but the milk's still sweet.

Act your age and not your sock size.

Strain'n at a gnat and swallowin' a camel. (Inconsistent or wishy washy)

Cacklin' like a bunch of hens.

He's so lazy he won't swat the flies off.

Moves as if the dead lice were falling off.

Too lazy to work and too nervous to steal.

Happy as a dead hog in the sunshine.

Happy as a pig in a poke.

How ya feeling? "Tolerable."

He thinks more of her than a pack mule does of a bell-mare.

I feel as common as dirt and as old as a rock.

He don't give two wraps and a hooey. (Calf roping expression—as in "wrapping" calves legs. Hooey is a knot.)

More nerve than a high diver.

Don't give two whoops and a holler.

Hotter'n a six shooter.

Hotter'n a two dollar pistol.

Hotter'n a depot stove.

Hotter'n high school love.

Poker-faced.

A faint heart never filled a flush.

That's the first rattle out of the box. (Dice shooters' expression.)

He's so honest, I'd shoot dice with him over the telephone.

He's a lover, a fighter, and a wild bull rider guaranteed not to rip, rattle, roll down hill and smell bad in hot weather.

He knows as much about that as a hog knows about a sidesaddle.

He hasn't got enough sense to pour rainwater out of a boot with the directions written all over the heel.

He knows as much about that as a hog knows about a buggy whip.

He doesn't know if he's washin' or hangin' out.

He doesn't know sic 'em from fetch 'em.

Dumb as Cooter Brown.

Not enough sense to come out of the rain.

He's so slow he can't catch cold.

I wouldn't trust him as far as I could throw him.

Rougher than bark on a tree.

Rough as a cob.

Quiet as a thief in a chicken house.

Smellier'n a wet dog.

Slick as Peter's heel. (Sly, untrustworthy)

Slick as owl grease.

He worked as hard as a cold-nosed bird dog.

He's snake-bit. (Had lots of bad luck)

Doesn't amount to a hill of beans.

Stand outside and let the stink blow off.

That's bigger'n Dallas.

I've known him since Trigger was a colt.

Batting eyes like a frog in a hailstorm.

That fits him a little quick.

Layover to catch meddlers. (Mind your own business)

Hell-bent for leather. (In a hurry)

Pick 'em up and lay 'em down.

Traveled faster'n bad news at a church social.

Be there in a New York minute. (Be there real fast)

It will never be noticed on a galloping horse.

That is like jumping out of the skillet into the frying pan.

Quicker than a minnow could swim a dipper.

Skeedaddle. (Move fast)

Lit a shuck. (Leave in a hurry—refers to corn shucks burning fast)

Hot to trot.

He could run like small town gossip.

Look for me when you see me comin'.

Faster'n greased lightening.

Faster'n a heart beat.

No flies on that one.

Eat my dust.

Shake a hoof.

Green as a gourd.

Mosey on over.

Always sucking the hind tit.
(Slow)

I got to get back to my rat killin'.

Everyone to his own taste, the old woman said as she kissed the cow.

He's humped up like a country girl on an organ stool.

As welcome as a pardon to a lifer.

Can't beat it with a stick.

Texas vittles. (Food)

A-fixin' dinner. (Texans "fix" a meal)

Larrupin' meal. (Good meal)

Saucered and blowed. (A cup of coffee)

Gimme a shot of up and attum. (Good strong coffee)

Puttin' the feed bag on. (To eat)

Grub wagon.

That's the best you ever locked your lip on.

A pair to draw to.

He's so tight he squeaks when he walks.

Tight as bark on a bois d'arc tree.

As tight as a fat lady's stocking.

He's so tight he's still got half his third grade allowance.

Tighter than a fat man's shoelaces.

Tighter'n a cinch strap.

He wears his pockets high off the ground. (Tall man)

She ain't ankle high to a June bug. (Short girl)

She ain't big as a minute.

He'd have to stand up to look a snake in the eye.

He doesn't know if he's getting off or getting on.

He was behind the door when the brains were passed out.

His bread ain't burnt yet. (Dumb)

Not worth a plug nickle.

Useless as teats on a boar hog.

Talk turkey.

Hungrier'n a woodpecker
with a sore pecker.

Hungrier'n a woodpecker with a headache.

He's so hungry his stomach thinks his throat's been cut.

Full as a tick.

Long, tall and hollow. (Never gets full)

I didn't just fall off a tater truck.

Do you think I just got to town
on a load of watermelons?

He could screw up an anvil.

Crazy as a hoot owl.

Nutty as a fruit cake.

Nutty as a bucket of pecans.

Tater diggin' thing.

Excited as a bug in a tater patch.

Helpless as a fart in a whirlwind.

Lonesome as a preacher on a payday.

Lower'n a snake's belly.

Lower'n a snake's belly in a wagon rut.

He felt so low he could sit on a cigarette paper and dangle his legs off the side.

That's a can of peaches.

In a pig's eye you will.

Does a chicken have lips?

Don't that blow your dress up?

Does a cat have a climbing gear?

Wouldn't that cock your pistol?

Don't that knock your hat in the creek?

Does a 50 lb. sack of flour make a big biscuit?

Is a snake's ass low to the ground?

Is a pig's ass pork?

It's so dry the catfish are wearin' flea collars.

It's so dry my catfish have ticks.

It's so dry my four year old duck doesn't know how to swim.

When the Good Lord sent the flood all we got was a quarter of an inch.

I remember when it never rained.

Five miles to water, six inches to hell. (Little or bad water.)

It's so dry on my place the bushes follow the dogs around.

Too wet to plow.

That was a real gully washer. (Hard rain)

Frog strangler. (Heavy rain)

Paying the wrong preacher. (No rain)

There is nothing between Texas and the North Pole but a bobwire fence.

So windy his whipping shirt sleeves wore blisters on his arms.

Colder than a well digger in Montana.

Cold as a witch's tit.

Cold enough to freeze the horns off a Billy Goat.

Blue Norther.

When a big storm hits, it is said "someone dropped the bobwire fence."

It's so hot the mosquitoes carry canteens.

Hot enough to cook an egg on the sidewalk.

Hotter'n hell.

In Texas none but fools and strangers predict the weather. If you don't like the weather, just wait a minute.

She's cute as a speckled pup.

She's pretty as a speckled pup under a new red wagon.

She's a cute little outfit.

Banjo legged. (Bow legged)

Don't wart me.

She'd take first place in halter class.

He looks like forty miles of bad road.

So ugly she looks like she was weaned on a pickle.

Ugly as a mud fence.

Ugly as homemade sin.

Ugle as homemade soap.

Looks like she was whipped with an ugly stick.

She's so ugly she'd have to sneak up on a drink of water.

She's so ugly she'd kill corn knee high.

She's so ugly she'd scare day into night.

His wife is so ugly he'd rather stay home than kiss her goodbye.

She could eat corn off the cob through the keyhole.

When he looked up ugly in the dictionary, there was her picture.

She looks like she could bite a hog on the ass through a picket fence.

Her hair looks like the back of Hannah's cat.

She ain't nothin' to write home about.

You changed everything about me but my name.

Give it a lick and a promise.

Hit the sack. (Go to bed)

You're lookin' awful temporary. (Not staying long)

Hot will cool if greedy will let it. (Be patient—refers to eating hot food)

All I need is a little time and a few kind words.

Too much sugar for a dime.

That's how the cow ate the cabbage.

Sweeter than a baby's breath.

As clear as Texas water.

Coon's age. (Long time)

Pocket full of nits. (Unimportant)

It's hard to get all your possums up one tree. (Descriptive of effort)

Cock and bull story.

His dog wouldn't bite a biscuit.

Head 'em up—move 'em out.

Sore as a scalded pup.

His voice is so low you can smell socks on his breath.

Rattles like a BB in a box car.

Rougher than a wood rasp.

So hard a cat couldn't scratch it.

Some Texans think "manual labor" is a Mexican.

Red River water—too thick to drink, too thin to plow.

Tender as an old maid's heart.

Stronger than battery acid.

Harder than Chinese arithmetic.

They scattered like a covey of quail.

That hit the nail on the head.

She don't think that old dog will hunt. (Won't be satisfied with or unacceptable)

Up a creek without a paddle.

Gutty as a government mule.

Wild as a peach orchard boar.

Clumsy as a bull in a china closet.

Hold your horses.

You can lead a horse to water, but don't push him in, 'cause there's nothing smells worse than a wet horse.

Can't ride a stick horse to water.

That horse was so bad, I couldn't tie my britches to him.

Don't change horses in the middle of the stream.

Jug head horse.

You can lead a horse to water but you can't make him drink.

He don't cotton to that. (Doesn't like)

Fair to middlin'. (Reply as to how you're feeling)

Much obliged. (Grateful)

Lucky enough to throw marbles in a swinging jug.

Nervous as a long-tailed cat in a room full of rocking chairs.

Nervous as a frog in a hot skillet.

A man afoot is no man at all.

Nothin' to write home about.

Be particular. (Be careful)

Dropped him like a hot potato.

Higher than a cat's back.

Well, I'll be John Brown.

Don't that take the rag off the bush! (Expression of astonishment)

I'll be hornswoggled.

I'll be dumbfounded.

His family tree was a scrub.

Howdied and shook. (Acquainted)

I've been back under the hen house lookin' for eggs further than you've been away from home.

As much chance as a snowball in hell.

I didn't stutter. (You heard what I said)

Enough to make a preacher cuss.

It will be a cold day in Hell. (Or in July)

Well, I'm fixin' to . . .

Chewin' the fat. (Talkin')

Ride shanks mare. (Walk)

Ridin' herd. (Watch over)

Finer'n frog hair.

Harder'n nails.

Forked end down. (Stand on your own two feet)

Make yourself useful as well as ornamental.

May all your babies be born nekkid and may you die of old age.

That's more fun than watchin' a nearsighted rooster in a hen house.

He throws a big loop. (Takes a lot of territory)

He can talk the horns off a Billy Goat.

Swelled up like a poisoned pup.

Pull yourself up by the bootstraps.

That would be easier than trying to sneak dawn past a rooster.

Never kick a dog or refuse a drink.

In Texas you can look farther and see less than anywhere in the world.

Get along little dogie, get along. (Dogie is a motherless, scrubby calf or one whose papa ran off with another cow)

Ain't exactly barefoot. (He's got some money)

Eatin' high on the hog. (Prosperous)

He's in mighty high cotton.

He had more money than Tom Mix had hats.

Ain't exactly cuttin' his own hair.

He's got enough money to burn up a wet dog.

He's so poor he can't pay attention.

Poor as Job's turkey.

He shot his wad. (Broke)

He was so crooked he had to screw on his socks.

He was so crooked that he couldn't sleep in a fence corner.

He was so crooked that you couldn't tell by his tracks which way he was going.

Crooked as a dog's hind leg.

He was so crooked they had to screw him in the ground when they buried him.

Crooked as a barrel of snakes.

Cotton Eyed Joe.

Kicker. (A Texan who dances good)

Boot scootin'. (Dancin')

Joober in the heel and devil in the heart. (Man and woman dancing together)

I'm gonna dance with him that brung me.

Skinny as a rail.

He's so skinny, if he stuck out his tongue, he'd look like a zipper.

She'd have to stand twice to make a shadow.

Not any bigger than a bar of soap after a hard day's washing.

She's so skinny she doesn't have enough ass to stink.

She's so skinny she'd have to run around in the shower to get wet.

She's so skinny she looks like she traded legs with a killdee and got cheated.

It takes a mighty big woman to weigh a ton.

Big as a No. 3 washtub.

She's a heavy springer. (Real pregnant)

Broader than the side of a barn.

She has more curves than a sack full of rattlesnakes.

Fat as a town dog.

She's so fat when she walks away it looks like two little boys fighting under the bedsheets.

He'd have to stick out an arm to see if he's walkin' or rollin'.

If she had to haul ass, it'd take two loads.

It took all hands and the cook. (Great effort)

Pert nigh but not plumb. (Nearly right)

Burnin' sunshine. (Wasting time)

Bite the dust.

Aim. (I aim to go)

Wait 'til hell freezes over.

Up to snuff.

Gotta bamoose. (Vamoose)

Dumb as a fence post.

Say hello and you hear an echo.

He doesn't know gee from haw.
(Old mule driving
expression—right from left)

He stood around like a big-eyed
goose.

Only time he opens his mouth is
to change feet.

Big as a tree or treetop tall.

Built (or stacked) like a brick
outhouse.

Ass high to a tall Indian.

If a frog had wings he wouldn't bump his bottom every time he jumped.

If a table had wheels, it'd be a teacart.

If a frog had wings he'd be a bird.

If that wouldn't hair lip the Governor.

If the Lord meant for Texans to ski, he'd have made bullshit white.

If I tell you a horse can lay a golden egg, better build him a nest.

If I tell you a chicken can pull a freight train, you better clear the tracks.

If I tell you a chicken can dip snuff, look under his wing and there'll be the can.

If it had been a snake it would have bit you.

If you're waitin' for me, you're backin' up.

He has too many irons in the fire.

Don't know if he's walkin' or horseback.

Busier than a one-legged man in an ass kickin' contest.

Busier than a cat coverin' up his evidence.

Busy as a barefoot boy in an ant bed.

Busier than a one-armed paperhanger.

Like a settin' hen on a June bug.

Anything is easy if you know what you're doing or you have the money.

You oughta saw . . .

He done good . . .

Never put yourself in a position where you have to have a real job or act your age.

Sweatin' like a mule.

Softer than a calf's ear.

Fire and Damnation man. (Preacher)

Goat roper. (Cowboy type)

Yellow dog Democrat. (Would vote for a yellow dog if he's a Democrat)

Ring tailed tooter.

Cussed runt.

Maverick. (Unbranded animal)

Bad guys in Texas are—varmints, sidewinders, back shooters, snake-in-the-grass, yellow-bellied, snake oil salesman.

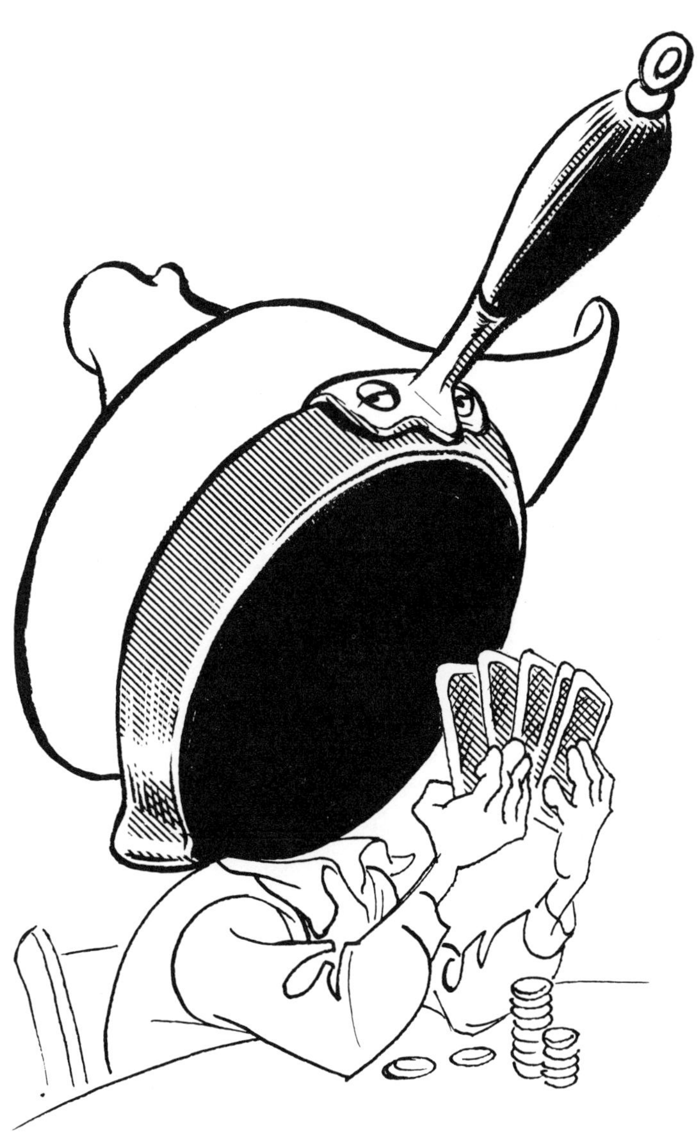

Dead-pan face.

Better'n sliced bread.

Put the quietus on that.

How bout them apples?

A faint heart never won a fair lady.

Have you got a mouse in your pocket?

He'll take you for a cleanin'.

He's so bowlegged he couldn't catch a pig.

Gaddin' about.

I can get up on that top shelf. (I can do that anytime)

Welcome as rain.

Worthless as a milk bucket under a bull.

Never was a horse that couldn't be rode—never was a man that couldn't be throwed.

Cinch buster. (Horse that rears and falls backwards)

That horse is spooky or boogery. (Horse that is easily scared)

He's got good horse sense.

Women are unlike horses; the wilder they are the easier they are to pet.

It's no use to beat a dead horse.

APPROVED TEXAS CUSSIN'

Dod Rosset	Goll Dern
Heck Fire	Garden Seed
Dad Skim	Shoot
Jiminy Christmas	Oh, Bull
Shoot Fire	Baloney Sausage
Bull Corn	Dad Burnit
Oh, Foot	Dad Blast it
Dang	Hells Bells
Dad Gum	Son of a Gun
Shucks	Dag Nabit

If we've left out your favorite expression send it to TEXAS TALKIN', P.O. Box 261, Argyle, Texas 76226. We will include it in our next book.